PSYCH / WARD

My Personal Experience With Bipolar, Psychosis, Catatonia, and Extra Pyramidal Symptoms Including Akathisia.

By Jade Nicoletti

Psych Ward

My Personal Experience with Bipolar, Psychosis, Catatonia and Extra Pyramidal Symptoms

Including Akathisia

By:

Jade Nicoletti

Cover design by [Jade's 12-year-old son]

First Edition: 2024

DEDICATION

I dedicate this book to my four beautiful children who are each truly my heart walking outside of my body. I give special mention to my one son (you know who you are) who helped me design the cover of this book (at age 12)! I also dedicate this book to my mom and dad who have housed me in tough times.

TABLE OF CONTENTS

I'm writing this book to make the subject of mental health less taboo. I figured if I came out with my personal experience of being hospitalized in the Psychiatric Ward not only once but four times, that people who are in a similar dilemma will be able to relate and hopefully find camaraderie, if not comfort. It is important that this subject become destigmatized so that those suffering from it can be treated like any other patient suffering from any other disease. It is sad to see what people diagnosed with a mental illness have to go through other than the illness itself because of misconceptions. I hope people reading this book will get a real dose of what it is like.

I have divided this book into four sections - one for each hospital stay. That way, the reader can compare the differences in how each state deals with mental health patients. There are definitely sharp contrasts from being treated like a prisoner to being treated like a patient, and some states do it better than others. There definitely needs to be reform to treat all mental patients like what they are - patients and not prisoners!

PREFACE

My childhood was crazy growing up in Utah with a Fundamentalist Polygamist family background, but I'll save that for another book. I was raised by my grandma and my "grandpa" - the man she married once my biological grandpa died.

There is a history of mental illness in my family, but for everyone's privacy, I'm not going to say who because those are their stories. At one point while growing up, my grandparents did have me put on psychiatric drugs because they said I was seeing things; however, these were just ordinary shadows and a big imagination. I still had to live with the weight gain pills packed on me until I went off of them as a teenager, which did affect my ability to make friends at school.

My married life, however, after leaving the cult and finding Christ, was normal prior to the hospitalizations. I was an Army Wife for the first five years. I held a job as a manager at a prominent health & bodybuilding store as well as a few other jobs during the first part of my marriage. Once I had baby number one at age

21, I continued working. Baby number two came nineteen months later, and I had planned to go back to work, but the day before, I got a phone call that I had no job to go back to. This started my venture in being a stay-at-home mom with the exception of one short part-time job I held for six months. Towards the end of 2010, we found out that I was expecting again - this time with twins!

IDAHO

There I was in the maternity ward waiting for my turn to be whisked back for a c-section. I had gone into pre-mature labor two nights before and they had given me medication to reverse it and a steroid shot to further the development of my identical twins' lungs. It was now the 35th week mark in my pregnancy. It was Saturday and I had been scheduled for my c-section on Monday but found myself in the hospital early with pre-eclampsia. One nurse said I was "Third Spacing" and lifted up my leg to show the other nurse how it had become dead weight swollen like I found the lower half of my body to now be up to the middle of my stomach. I could no longer void and all the IV fluid had no place to go since my bladder was full and was now accumulating in these third spaces in my body causing the swelling is the best way my non medically certified self can explain it. The hospital was full that weekend as every pregnant woman in the city seemed to be in labor on the same day. The surgery suite was no exception and the doctors had been at it all day with emergency c-sections that took precedence over a pre-eclamptic woman who was third spacing. Finally, towards the end of the day they took me back for the surgery.

Besides the needle they stick in your back for the anesthetic feeling like I was being stabbed with a knife the surgery went well. Baby A and Baby B were cleaned up after I got to briefly view them and then they were whisked away to NICU since they were five weeks premature but overall healthy. My husband then shortly after had to leave for home to take care of our other two children. I was left alone to recover at the hospital with my two new babies who were now a floor above me almost directly situated above my room. Recovery was going very smoothly. I was now no longer pregnant with twins which meant I had room to breathe again and the swelling was going down from the third spacing and now I could also pee again. My body seemed to actually be functioning. I was doing so well the nurses were commenting on how I hardly seemed like I had just had a c-section with twins, but to me it felt like the weight of the world was lifted off my shoulders. I figured in my head that God must have given me an extra amount of energy to be able to care for two babies. It did slow slightly as I was showering after and pulled a muscle in my shoulder. The well-meaning nurses must have said something to the hospital social worker about me being up and about because the social worker paid me a visit and cautioned me that my babies needed me and was very vague otherwise In regards to what she said. I translated it as I needed to do more for them only to find out later in this story that she meant quite the opposite that I needed to take it easy and recover. Things further spiraled out of control when I was not told that the babies would be fed in NICU thinking I had to be there round the clock every two hours to breast feed them.

The day came for the staples to be removed from my stomach. I was nervous about it as I had never had staples removed before. She told me oh it's only like a small bee sting. She couldn't have told me anything worse! I'm terrified of bees also because I have never been stung by one and don't know what it is like. She offered me a pain killer beforehand to help with any pain. She was right about the staples not being much of an issue except for a couple stubborn ones, but it sure didn't take long for me to have a massive headache like a pencil had been jabbed into my head and was running from one side to the other, I could now hear an acute dripping of the faucet like it was magnified in a speaker and I lay down not able to do anything as my breathing became shallower and shallower and my blood pressure skyrocketed. My nurse assured me that it couldn't have been the pain killer. Shift after shift my blood pressure wasn't coming down till my nurse flat out told me that she was required to be with me because of it but couldn't because she had other patients to attend to and left. After a couple days it subsided. It had been the first time that I was actually so sick I was stuck in bed and couldn't make it up to the NICU. I can't remember why, maybe it was a headache but the nurse offered me the same pain killer a second time and I was hesitant because of what I had just been through. She assured me it wasn't the pain killer and stupidly I took it a second time only for a repeat of the symptoms to happen all over again. My breathing was so shallow one night I was sure that if I went to sleep, I would quit breathing in my sleep and wake up dead. The end of the week was approaching and I was set to be released from the hospital as my insurance only paid for a one week stay. I begged my doctor for more time and he deeply apologized and said he wished he could but insurance wouldn't allow it.

My husband picked me up from the hospital leaving the twins behind in NICU. I continued to venture to the NICU as often as we could to breastfeed round the clock only this time, I knew they were feeding them with a high calorie formula in between feedings. I continued to get sicker and sicker. My body was becoming accustomed to being awake around the clock. Soon I couldn't sleep if I wanted to. I stayed up cleaning the house at all hours of the night while my husband slept preparing for the babies' arrival at the apartment. When I went shopping, I came across a nurse from the hospital that couldn't believe I was out shopping let alone carrying everything in my arms without a cart. I was barely doing it but I was doing it, what else was I going to do to pass the time. Plus, my kids needed coats for winter and I didn't know when I would have the time to shop once the babies came home. At the grocery store, a kind man helped me in the produce isle and then again, another man with bagging groceries. I began to wonder if he was my guardian angel because both men looked identical. I ran into the drug store and my husband was getting irritated with me or the kids or both. I was going in to spend some money on baby items since I didn't have time for a baby shower before I went into labor. I had intended to go in by myself but out of frustration my husband sent our three-and-a-half-year-old and five-year-old in with me. They wanted to buy stuff for the twins too and started tossing baby toys in the cart faster than I could say no. I decided not to take away their joy. Needless to say, my husband wasn't happy with the receipt and returned the items the next day. We were eating out too, too exhausted to make food. The grilled chicken sandwich at our local fast-food restaurant had becomes my favorite. That and the "healthy" chocolate bars I was buying in the natural food store for their "iron" content since I always become anemic after childbirth. I do remember attempting a dine in restaurant and no sooner did we get set at a table then I had to go back out to the SUV because my head was spinning and I felt sick. My husband bought fries for the kids and brought them back out in a to go box. It wasn't long after that I would ask my husband if the sink counter top was crooked because the water seemed to roll off the counter and the room was beginning to look crooked as well. That wasn't the only new development with my health. I had begun to foam at the mouth and I was insisting that the drugs they had given me in the hospital must have poisoned me. My husband was becoming very concerned and didn't know what to do because of my lack of sleep so he contacted the hospital social worker. That ended up being one of the worst things he could have done.

The social worker advised him to have me evaluated at the hospital for my mental health and he told her I wouldn't be willing to do that so she told him to call the police on me and have them meet me at the hospital the next time I visited the NICU. So, he set that up. He was overly frustrated with me that day because I was taking my sweet time loading up the SUV with things, we would need for NICU. I included my cross-stitch blanket I was working on for my older son. I was dilly dallying this day so he went ahead of me and called me on the phone to come in from the SUV to the maternity ward. I instinctively knew something was up when I walked in and went to the stairs to "hide". I then checked myself in as a visitor to the maternity floor and put their sticker on my shirt that said I was supposed to be there. That is where my husband met up with me with the cops. They said, we need to talk to you and took me aside to an empty room. Now at this point I knew what was up. When I was a child, a person close to me in my family was taken away to the psych ward by police officers and then the rest of the family disowned her. I couldn't believe that that was what my husband was about to do to me. I took my time trying to explain to the officers how I was normal and even held up the cross-stitch blanket that I was working on for my son. Inside though I was dying a thousand deaths as I spoke trying to plead my innocence. I couldn't believe my husband would betray me like this. They finally said will you be willing to go to the hospital to be evaluated and I told them that I never should have left the hospital in the first place because I was sick and that I would be willing to go.

Stepping foot into the emergency room was my breaking point. I figured my husband was no longer going to love me and it caused an actual mental breakdown. They placed me in a room and put a guard outside my door to keep me from leaving. I told them how I was still sick from my hospital stay and handed them a vial that I had collected of my mouth foam insisting that if they tested it, they would see that I had been poisoned. That the pain killer and whatever else they had given me was a deadly combination of drugs. They sent someone in with a questionnaire and asked me a bunch of questions. I remember also having to pee a lot, more than usual and them thinking that was weird because the guard kept letting me out to use the bathroom. I told him in a not so lucid state if I won the lottery, I was going to give him money because he was an angel. The hospital staff also insisted that I had not been poisoned they said they had tested the vial twice. They then transported me (I don't remember how) to the Psych ward which was not by the hospital. My twins were still in NICU.

At the psych ward in Idaho, I was placed in a room with two beds. Again, a guard was posted outside of the door. I remember trying to get his attention so I would have someone to talk to only it came out a bit flirty and so I added my husband won't mind. It didn't work and I had nothing to do for once at this point so I actually rolled over in bed and fell asleep. I think a good night's sleep was all I needed because when I woke up, I was fine again but the nurse was disgusted with me and I asked her if something was wrong, if perhaps she didn't like my dress- it came above my knees and she says I was being inappropriate and should change. So, I changed into the hospital clothes. Walking by the nurse window, I saw the breathing apparatus they had given me to practice my breathing after the c-section and so I asked the nurse for it and she said I couldn't have it because it wasn't mine. I wandered off, at this point the guard was no longer by my door, and found the lunchroom. There was a table full of staff people and a bunch of crayons and colored pencils so I sat down and was gruffly asked to leave because it was the staff table. Soon it was lunch and I lined up with the rest of the people there to wait for the food like one does in a school cafeteria. I got my food and remembered to walk past the man who gruffly spoke to me. I found a table and sat down and ate. A little food and sleep do wonders for recovery. I think that was all I needed all along.

While I was in the Psych Ward, I met this girl named Kat. There was a girl named Kat who wrote dark poetry in Freak Alley which I loved reading and I wondered if she might be the same person. We soon became friends. She carried a stuffed puppy dog with her everywhere she went. She called him Henry. There was another girl there who looked vaguely familiar I wondered if I had gone to any homeschool functions with her growing up and she said she had. The three of us then went into the lunch room and saw this older woman with her two grown daughters and she seemed very afraid to be there. Kat assured them that we would watch over her and be like her guardian angels while she was there. There was a small grassy area outside the lunchroom that was fenced in. I was allowed out in it with a few other people. I contemplated jumping the fence and running away but knew I'd be caught by the police and brought back. Besides where would I go if I did since my husband abandoned me. I decided it would just be best to stick it out. Inside it was almost lunch again and I noticed this blind girl in line with her walking stick. I probably inappropriately asked her how she had become blind and she preceded to tell me how when she was suicidal, she shot herself in the head and lived but the outcome was that she was blind from it. Later on, I would learn she would have no family to return to either when she left the hospital. I also remember meeting a Middle Eastern man while I was there who I struck up a conversation with. I found out he was also a Christian like me. He ended up in the hospital because he had flipped a table over in anger at his house and his brother had called the cops on him.

After a few days I was informed that I had to go to court. Boy was I up for a surprise. Going to court entailed being shackled from head to toe with chains and cuffs. I was escorted out of the building and into the back of a cop car. We drove to mental health court. He opened the door to the cop car to let me out. I could barely move from the weight of the chains. I was also very weak and unsteady because at this point, I was anemic from the childbirth. I asked if I could take his hand to walk and he said I wasn't allowed to touch him. Inside they asked me if I had ever been inside a holding cell before. I had said no. So, they put me inside but left the door open guarding it. It wasn't long before the judge was ready to see me. The judge proceeded and the person next to me told me what I needed to do and say. Soon court was over and I was driven in the cop car back to the Psych ward.

Back at Psych I learned that the doctors are looking at whether you are participating in classes as a sign as to whether to release you. So, I remember attending an art class. I remember Kat watching tv one day and a news report came on about a girl she knew that had been murdered and she became very distraught. I tried to give her a hug and she told me hugs weren't allowed in the psych ward. She asked me to watch and see if they find out who did it and she went to talk to her family who had come to visit. I came and gave her the update. On the day Kat was actually released or sent on to another long-term hospital- I think it was the latter, she actually came and gave me a hug breaking the rule. The day finally came for doctors to be in the Psych ward and one pulled me aside to talk to him. I insisted that I needed to get home to feed my babies. He told me that he was filling in for my regular doctor and he thought that doctor wanted me to stay longer. I asked him if the medication was fine for breastfeeding and if I would be able to be pregnant on it because I don't believe in abortion. I don't remember what he said about the medication but that he understood because he was Catholic. I think the fact that we were both Christians might have helped in him actually releasing me because he didn't make me stick around for the other doctor who wanted me to stay longer. The nurse came by with a bunch of paperwork for me to sign and she was really agitated with me because I wanted to actually read through it before signing. She said it basically meant that I was required by law to take my medication for so many days and go to a psychiatrist or I would end up back in the hospital again.

The day came for me to be released and my husband was actually there to pick me up. It turns out the twins had been released from NICU like three days prior to me being released from Psych. I had been in the Ward for one week but it felt like forever.

SOUTH CAROLINA

The repercussions of my first hospital stay lingered. By court order I was required to take my medication and see a psychiatrist or risk going back to the psych ward. The med they prescribed me caused photosensitivity. Being that we only had one car at the time I had to walk my kids to school and myself to see the psychiatrist in the sunlight. My eyesight wasn't the only thing affected, there was still the fact that my husband had called the cops on his own wife, who had just birthed twins, for the reason of not sleeping. He would go on to tell me that I wouldn't go to the hospital which was ridiculous because I didn't want to leave the hospital in the first place because I knew something was wrong. Little did I know his calling the cops on me and my fear of that would lead me into a slight breakdown. We had relationship issues for about six months with me being mad at him for calling the cops on me. Had he just asked I would have gone to emergency albeit for being generally sick. I just didn't know insurance would cover that since I had asked for an extended stay in the maternity ward.

After my required time on the medication was over my psychiatrist told me it was up to me if I wanted to continue, which I did not. In my mind the break down was due to having twins in the NICU for three weeks (two of which I was there, one in the psych ward) and being there every two hours to feed them which caused lack of sleeping and lack of eating for me. The trigger was my husband calling the cops on me leading me to think he was abandoning me forever after that point. One night of sleep and only having to care about myself in the psych ward with a good meal brought me out of my brief breakdown. So, I chalked it up to that.

My husband was working outrageous hours (22 a day) and this at a very low unfair compensation. He only worked to further his skillset so he could move on but I was worried that this would do him in. His project eventually finished and he applied for a government contract job in South Carolina which paid the national average and he got it. The twins had just turned one.

We lived in South Carolina for three years and I believe I had been fine till year two or three. It all started with symptoms of anemia, but it was much more than that because I was feeling strange, sick-like. I had done The Alkaline Diet in the past and thought that might help me get better so I started myself on green drinks and would nap all the time with the twins while the older two were in school. I knew something wasn't right so I checked myself into urgent care because I was even having chest pain at this point. With them hearing that they moved me to the front of the line. Everything checked out fine, with the exception that I was extremely anemic. They said I was so anemic they were surprised I was even able to walk into the clinic. In hindsight they should have referred me to a hospital for a blood transfusion but didn't. I asked them before leaving if they were sure I wasn't pregnant and they assured me I wasn't. Time kind of warps when you're sick but I believe these green drinks, naps, and sickness continued on for another week with me only feeling sicker and sicker. I went to urgent care a second time with my husband this time and the tests came back the same the level on my anemia test had only improved by one point due to all my green drinks and I was again worried that I might be pregnant. To which again they assured me I wasn't.

I don't know how many days later it was but my husband was home and I was sitting in a chair. He was standing in front of me trying to talk to me but no words could come out of my mouth. I was mute and just blankly stared at him as he tried to understand and get me to talk to him. I couldn't and he knew something was wrong. He called some people we knew from the church to come watch the kids and another to drive us to the hospital in the city which he was unfamiliar with.

It was nighttime and the emergency rooms were full. I could talk again but only slightly. I saw these black elderly couple sitting in one of the curtained off areas on a chair with a suitcase. It reminded me of an old-time scene in history and I said, "Slaves." out loud although I meant no harm to it. The black nurse on duty heard me and told me I had to watch what I said in the emergency room. As we were waiting, I was sure my husband's cousin was in the next room over for drug use- which he wasn't. (Ironically later in life he would die to drug use.) Way late into the night a curtained off section came available for me. No psych doctors would be available until morning so I would be spending my night in the E.R. My husband left me to return home. As I lay on the hospital bed, I could see all the people in uniform, firefighters, policeman, EMT's rushing back and forth past my curtain. That with the sirens I was sure a war was going on. I finally fell asleep. At some point early in the morning someone said I could watch tv. I believe I just turned the power button on and watched the station it was on. It was on PBS on a nature show with beautiful scenery and birds. I envisioned couples in the form of shadows on the tv one of which was my sister and her husband and the other my husband and myself and I just knew we were meant to be together forever. As the credits rolled, I read names that were familiar and figured they might be talking about people I personally knew in life. I rested peacefully just watching these nature shows. When the sun came up, I sat up in my bed and just rocked back and forth with my arms wrapped around my legs which were crisscrossed. A male nurse walked in and asked me why I hadn't touched my breakfast which I hadn't even noticed was in the room. I replied and told him I was waiting for someone to come eat with me. Now nobody ever came to eat with me and I missed breakfast.

Now that it was morning, a doctor was finally available and he told me I would be being sent to the Psych Ward which was across the street and he would see me over there. A police officer handcuffed me and escorted me to his cop car. After being loaded into the back seat I asked him if he was sure he didn't want to shackle my feet as well since that is what they had done the last time I was in a police car. He laughed and said no. He took me to an entrance of the psych ward that led directly into the unit, uncuffed me, and sat me in a chair. Then he left. The first thing I noticed is the building smelled heavily of smoke (which it didn't, it was just an olfactory hallucination). I sat there thinking someone was going to come and get me but no one did. I eventually left my chair and wandered further into the ward. There was a giant "Welcome" sign in the center of it which I greatly appreciated. It was quite the contrast from the last psych ward I had been in. At some point a nurse came up to me with a clipboard to ask me some information. I think I was doing alright with the questions until she asked me where I was. I looked around at the brick walls and it reminded me of the hospital's walls that my older two children had been born in so I gave her that hospital's name. Upon failing this answer, she stared wide eyed and put her board down. Apparently, there would be no more questions.

Once again, the room I was assigned to had two beds. This time I had a big window and just my luck the cherry trees outside were blooming beautiful pink cherry blossoms. I left the room to attend group time. Everyone was seated in a circle and taking turns introducing themselves. For the most part everyone was ok. There was just one or two scary individuals. I tended to avoid the tv area because that is where they liked to hang out. Plus, the tv seemed to make me hallucinate. On my way past the tv area one day I could audibly hear lions roaring and even I knew I was hallucinating because I knew there was no way lions were in the psych ward. One of the days it was game & puzzle time and I was a bit manic going back and forth organizing the table. Then some menstrual cramps set in so I sat down. I was sure I was going into labor… but not just any labor that I was Mother Mary about to give birth to Jesus. I just sat in that chair and rocked and rocked until the cramps subsided and then I went about like nothing had happened. One day the guys were being loud and scary and my elderly roommate was scared so I started singing Amazing Grace to calm her down. I kept singing till she started to feel better. A nurse was in the room with us and she thanked me for singing.

There was only one phone in the building which all us patients had to share to call home. If you ever find yourself in this situation this is where having phone numbers memorized comes in handy because you are not allowed your cell phone. I was waiting my turn at the phone one day and this young man was using it dressed all fancy in a white suit and tie. I didn't know who he was but I got the impression that he came from a wealthy family and had money. Later that day at lunch his mom and dad came to visit him and he tried to introduce them to me as what sounded like a girl he liked. They just listened like they were aware they're in a psych ward and their son is not right in the head. I mean after all, how can someone from such a well to do family possibly have their son like a girl in the psych ward. Anyway, it didn't matter, we both were crazy and I was married. There was another young man I disappointed as well. It seemed he was interested in me until I told him he reminded me of my cousin. That put an end to that.

After one of our classes one day, they told us they were going to give us some time outside. The walk to the courtyard was far and as I passed the doctor on the way out, I told him I didn't feel good. He asked in what way thinking I was talking mentally. I told him I could barely walk because of the anemia. He just listened and I kept walking. In the courtyard surrounded by high stone walls and trees I found a sharp piece of metal. I handed it to one of the supervisors afraid someone might try to end their life with it if they found it. I then just enjoyed the rest of my time in the courtyard getting some fresh air and looking at flowers and trees.

I had been in the psych ward in South Carolina for I think two weeks before they finally released me. I had no visitors the entire time as my husband was watching the kids. This time the doctor put me on a new medication- a mood stabilizer. This medication would eventually kill my thyroid so to speak- it gave me hypothyroidism as a side effect.

WASHINGTON (PART ONE)

I can't remember if it was this newest medication or another drug, but I think it was the med. After we had moved to Washington in 2015 so my husband could get a better job, my primary physician there had told me he didn't like the psych drug I was on because it causes so much weight gain. He said he had an in-house Psychiatrist that I could go to and I could try going off of the drug to see how I do in the meantime. I was ok for a month or two. Then one of my close friends lost her four-year-old son in a roll over car crash and it hit too close to home because all our kids were about the same ages. In a couple weeks' time I found myself hallucinating at the tv and when my kids were making a mess in the kitchen, I found myself washing their feet with my wet hair to forgive them instead of disciplining them. The kitchen was left soaking wet. Soon my husband came home early from work because he was worried that because I hadn't texted him all day so he thought something might be off. He was right but I protested that he was wrong. He told me we were going to see the psychiatrist. On the way out the door I was checking the undersides of vehicles for car bombs while simultaneously explaining to him that he was the one that needed to see a psychiatrist or even better we needed a family session so we would all function better as a unit. He went into the psychiatrist's office only to be told we had to wait an hour or two before we could be seen so he drove us to an empty parking lot nearby and we waited.

It only took that one to two hours' time for things to go from bad to worse. By the time the appointment came with all four kids in tow, I could barely walk. It wasn't even baby steps; it was a slight shuffle. My husband told me I was embarrassing him as I tried my best to make it into the clinic. All four kids sat down in chairs in the waiting room and the doctor came out. My husband explained to him what was going on and my psychiatrist asked me if I knew his name. I was now also having trouble speaking I told him his name incredibly slowly and sounded out. He instructed my husband to take me to the emergency room where his fellow colleague worked because he was specialized and would know what to do. Years down the road my psychiatrist told me this was to rule out other problems with the brain that could be causing it. He also told me I didn't need to even go to a Psych Ward unless I was a threat to myself or others and yet my husband kept sending me there and would do it a total of four times.

After getting his uncle to babysit, we headed to the E.R. I remember sitting in the waiting room. I must have blacked out because the next thing I remember is lying on a gurney with a doctor prying my eyes open to shine a light in them. I believe my eyes were rolled back in my head because I didn't see the light directly. I found myself unable to move or speak- I was mute & my muscles were as stiff as a corpse. I was alive in a dead person's body and if it weren't for the psychosis I was simultaneously experiencing I would have been freaking out in my head.

At some point they moved me to a room. I started to come to but it was slow… at first. Once I started talking though I really started talking and I couldn't stop. Words were just flowing out of my mouth one after another and mostly in rhyme. It was like I had just discovered that I could talk again but had no control over shutting up. I looked over at my husband and he looked sick of it already. It took a while but the doctor came in and told us they would be transferring me to a Psyche Ward but there wasn't room yet and I'd have to stay at the main hospital until there was room. He wanted to know if my husband was going to drive me or if he should order an ambulance. I can't remember my reasoning exactly in the moment but it had to do with germs. I believe I was afraid if my husband took me, he would be taking home even more germs to our kids so I insisted that I had to go in the ambulance. My husband left and they transferred me to a room with glass windows to wait for the ambulance.

A nurse came in and I asked her if she had any food and she said she only had crackers. I agreed to the crackers and asked her if I could use the bathroom. She showed me that I had one behind a door in the room and could use it. I wanted to use the bathroom because I could suddenly smell myself and I smelled really bad and wanted to take a shower (It was another olfactory hallucination). There was no shower in the bathroom so I gave myself a sponge bath with wet paper towels. Once I was satisfactorily clean enough, I went back in the room. I noticed that there were colored lines running across the floor. The next time the nurse came in I told her that on this side of the line was my half of the room and on the other side of the line was her half of the room. She listened. As I waited for the ambulance, I looked through the glass window all across the room to screens I couldn't see very well on the wall and figured I was looking at airport travel screens- the ones that tells you the schedule of when the planes come in. I was also still somewhat paranoid when I saw them and was trying to get someone's attention for a security guard to no avail. After a while the ambulance finally arrived.

This was my first ambulance ride ever in my life. I can't be 100% certain but I believe they let me sit on a seat in the back that had a seat belt for the trip. I don't really remember the ride. I do remember the hospital room they led me to and it was huge with a view of the mountains and I had it to myself… well except for the guards that rotated some which sat outside it and some inside it with me.

I was certain that the male patient in the room across was one of the rescuers from a landslide in the area that was in the news and now he also found himself in the hospital. There was quite the commotion coming from his room and it sounded like he had either died or almost died and then started breathing again. My entertainment while I waited for a room in the Psych Ward to come available was listening to the nurses' conversations in the hallway. During the guards' shift change I got a young college girl. She might have actually been a nurse acting on behalf of a guard I'm not sure. She looked sad and I asked her about her life. She told me about how her grandpa had just died and some of her other burdens. I told her about Jesus and that if she gave her burdens to Him to hold that He would give her feathers in return to hold.

It was getting to be nighttime and the nurse said the doctor from the E.R. had ordered me yet another medication. I wanted her to make sure it was from the doctor I had seen so I had her double check. I also had the chance to look at a menu before the hospital kitchen closed for the night. I just don't recall if I had the chance to eat the food before the next ambulance arrived to take me to the Psych Ward.

Two young men with a stretcher came to get me and loaded me onto the bed making sure my toes were covered with blankets and I was warm. As they wheeled me out, I could hear them chatting with one another about the miracles they had seen take place on the job. Once inside the ambulance it was dark and as it drove quickly into the night, I was amazed at how quickly they got me across the city. I either fell asleep or blacked out because the next thing I remember is waking up in a strange room with a person in another bed next to me with their back turned towards me. A nurse instructed me about the linens and towels I could use that were in the room and then she called me out into the hall. I could barely walk. She told me I needed to fill out this form that listed who was allowed to visit me. An easy enough task, right? Wrong. In my head I was certain that my friend whose son had passed had one of my kids and I (or my husband in this case) had one of hers. As I wrote my husband's and kids names down one by one, I struggled with the last one not knowing who had who. The Holy Spirit stepped in and helped me with this one letting me know he had her kid and my husband had ours and I was able to complete the form with the correct names. It was the middle of the night, so I walked back to my room and went to bed after they had given me my new medications.

I woke up feeling refreshed having had the best sleep ever asking the nurse what they had given me. It had actually stopped my thoughts from running rampant in my head allowing me to sleep and a full night at that. It was a Benzodiazepine. It had also improved my walking ability. I felt like me again!

I wandered around the Psych Ward. It was very beautiful and newly constructed. It had these marble-like pillars in the center of it next to the tables and book shelves. There was also a tv that when it wasn't being used as a tv they would put up nature pictures and videos with nature sounds. I would soon learn this was because they had no outside area for their patients. This would eventually become agitating because after too long being literally locked indoors I was missing fresh air and sunshine and blue sky (as blue as you can get for Seattle anyway- the sky is usually gray.) I sat down close to a girl who had bandages around her wrists. It would take me several days to realize that that was because she had probably been cutting her wrists. I met other interesting people in the Psych Ward as well. There was this very lively middle-aged man who had no legs in a wheelchair who I struck up a friendship with. It seemed as though he had already created a friend group, but we became friends anyway. There was this elderly lady that was always complaining about her feet. She had some kind of condition that bothered them, diabetes perhaps, and was mad at the doctors for taking away her shoes. There was an elderly man from Africa. A young blonde who liked to color. A man in his thirties who was always hitting on me. A dude who always yelled and slammed doors because he was mad, he was in there and his friend. An old Asian woman who didn't speak English who they allowed to stay in her room with her family probably for that exact same reason. And then there was Red. A man in his late twenties who was actually homeless and had feigned to be crazy so he could get warm food to eat and a bed to sleep in. People called him Red because of the color of his hair.

The next time I saw the elderly lady's doctor I asked him to get her shoes because her feet were in pain. He agreed to but said it had to be without the laces. She was happy and I heard no more complaining. Each day I would spend with my new found friends. The man in the wheelchair was friendly and we always talked daily. As time wore on though and his medications took affect that would cease. He was no longer lively and he no longer wanted to talk to me. It was like he was a changed person and became a shell of himself.

At lunch the food was good but not as good as it was at the other wards, I had been in. One day to my disgust, I found a dead bug in my salad! Red would always complain loudly about the quality of the food and how they would often get his order wrong. He would also quickly eat up any of the food anyone had left on their plates that they didn't want. I didn't know if it was his medication that was making him so hungry or the fact that he was homeless- probably both. I often didn't know what to order for dessert. Among other desserts it gave me the option of Angel Food Cake or Devil

Food Cake and I was under the impression that I had to pick based on my behavior for the day. Some days I just didn't know how I had behaved so I would circle both and put a question mark next to it. To my surprise when I would do this, they would bring me out both desserts to eat at once!

After lunch, I sat down at another table with an older woman I don't remember much about. What I do remember however is Red brought over two heated blankets he had rolled up and placed them around the backs of each of our necks and down onto our shoulders! I was moved at such a kind action and delighted at the discovery that the hospital had a blanket warmer and learned you just had to ask for one. I also found that the hospital had a scale in the room where you could get toiletries but it was accessible with a nurse only. I found myself quickly losing weight each time I weighed. Speaking of toiletries, the drain to the shower in that my roommate and I shared was clogged. I would always go into use the toilet and find a soaking wet floor. When I took a shower myself, I would lay towels on the floor just past the drain to soak up any excess water that didn't go down. This would always leave a pile of drenched towels that I had to carry to the dirty linen bin outside of my room. I finally reported it and after a while they sent a repairman to fix it.

There were plenty of things to do in this hospital. There was a computer room where I could log in and check my email and my Facebook. When I wasn't doing that, I could read from the many assorted books on the bookshelf. I found the Bible and highlighted my favorite verses in it. This would come in handy later, as the man who was hitting on me one day started questioning which religion was right and I was able to pull the Bible off the bookshelf and hand it to him showing him

John 3:16 about God loving the world and sending Jesus to die on the cross forgiving us for our sin and John 1:1 & 14 which shows that Jesus is God. He seemed to take it all in and took the Bible with him. One of my favorite things to do in this hospital was actually something Red showed me. At the end of each hall was a solitary room that had lights in it and possibly music but I believe you had to ask the front desk for that to be turned on. I would sit in this room and watch the lights change color and in different patterns and it would fascinate me and be so relaxing. I would come in here day after day and not many people even knew about it or at least chose to use it so it was usually empty. On chance it was full I would go to the one at the end of the other hallway. And then of course there were the classes. At the exercise class it was like I had no issues with movement anymore and was back to my old self and I mastered it like I typically did the fitness classes back home. My favorite class though was art. Once again Red mastered the music system in that room and we would rock out while doing art projects. I did so many I got in trouble for not saving their limited supplies for other patients.

One day I was talking to the man from Africa. I don't remember which country he was from. He said he had a prophecy for me. That one day I myself and my children would be in Africa. I am not one to shy away from prophecy especially ones given to me personally, so I noted it in my head. This man was nice and kind and didn't at all seem crazy. On the other hand, though, the man who was hitting on me had all these grandiose thoughts about who he was and how important he was and that he was like a spy or something trying to impress me and wondering why I wasn't impressed kind of getting angry about it. I finally complained at the front desk and they made sure he wasn't by me again. He wasn't the only one angry though, the first man I told you about that was angry and his friend, I overheard them talking one night in the hallway about how they had taken away his knife that he had and he knew the cupboard they had stored it in and were going to break into it and escape the Psyche Ward. I was very afraid and asked the nurse to lock me in my room for the night. She assured me I was safe and that they did rounds on patients' rooms checking them every fifteen minutes. Well, it didn't take long for the angry man and his friend to start causing a ruckus in the hallway arguing with staff and trying to break things. That same nurse swiftly came back and shut my door. Upon waking in the morning, I found a broken cupboard in the main room and I didn't see the man. I believe he had been taken away by security.

It came time for me to see the doctor or in other words time to prove to him that I was sane so I could leave. I probably talked too much but hopefully not too fast (they look for that kind of thing) and among other things said to him how my husband and I like to donate to charities and help the poor. I somehow thought that might help my chances of getting out. I also for the first time ever in a Psych Ward had visitors! My husband had brought the children to see me. The doctor took us all to a separate room that was safe for kids and brought them paper to color on and crayons. There were also some large soft foam furniture blocks and shapes they could play on and rock on. It was so refreshing to see my kids! The visit didn't last long before they were becoming restless like little kids do and finally had to leave. I found out I was going to be released soon and also discovered that the Ward had a washer and dryer so I washed my clothes I had come in with (I had been wearing the paper or whatever it is clothes they give you when you don't have any as I typically did with my stays). In the evening, I found Red and another person in a movie room that was on the side that had couches. He asked me if I wanted to watch a movie and I said yes and I told him about how I was going to be released. He knew how to skateboard and I always wanted for my kids to learn so I asked him for his number and if he would mind teaching them some stuff. He was fine with it especially when I mentioned that there was an Indian restaurant next to the skate park we could go to as well. (Once I was out though and tried calling his phone, I never got through to him. So that was the last I heard or seen of Red.)

The day had come for me to be released. The doctor had put me on a new antipsychotic. I was also still taking my Benzo daily. As I waited for my husband to pick me up, I sat next to the blonde girl who was coloring. Her parents had just brought her some new coloring supplies and a bunch of flowers in a plastic purplish vase. I sat with her awhile and watched her color. After a bit I went up to the counter by the front desk to wait (It was closer to the doors to leave.) The blonde girl soon followed me up to the counter with the flowers and handed them to me and left. I thought it was a nice gesture until I got looking at them closer and found that the bouquet was full of tiny bugs! After about an hour or so my husband arrived with kids in tow and we headed out of the hospital and home. I had been in this Psych Ward two weeks.

The first two or three weeks on the antipsychotic my head was definitely different. I was bedridden just stuck in my head. It's hard to explain. I was out of it and I couldn't even think thoughts. It's like the thoughts in my head were just a mass of the color gray. Thankfully, after I got adjusted to it this went away and I started functioning again… for a while. Come about three to four months later in October and November I started having weird symptoms. I was driving my daughter to a birthday party around Halloween and my hands started shaking and contorting into weird stiff shapes. I was able to drive home but didn't feel safe driving after that. This started a season of my body not being able to sit down. I would sit down just to have to stand back up. My body needed to just pace from one side of our small apartment to the other over and over again sometimes run. When I wasn't running, I was marching in place with my arms and hands shaking up and down and contorting into different stiff positions. At night I couldn't sleep well. I would lay awake with my legs moving back and forth and if I was lucky, I would fall asleep. This was my only respite but it wouldn't last long.

I went to my local Psychiatrist (the one that referred me to his buddy at the hospital). He started dosing me down on the antipsychotic and put me on a new drug but the damage was already done and then some. I was only on this new drug for about a week. It was giving me panic attacks (the first I had ever had in my life and they were extreme) as well as suicidal thoughts. I was constantly thinking of death. Even when my husband was looking at new cars to buy, I sat in one and I couldn't quit thinking of how it reminded me of a hearse and how I would soon be needing one. My psychiatrist took me off the drug immediately. And told me to dose down again on the antipsychotic since my symptoms weren't improving. He told me it looked like I was experiencing Akathisia. With each step down in dose it became more impossible to sleep. My symptoms weren't improving so I began researching Akathisia online and found only a few videos on it on YouTube posted by people who had it or their loved ones. Most of them were adamant against doctors and especially suddenly starting or stopping a new medication. I was afraid to go back to the doctor and but I continued dosing down on the antipsychotic. This in turn continued shortening my sleep span with each decrease till I was down to between zero and two hours of sleep per night. Instead of the slight respite of sleep I had for my symptoms at night, I would now lay awake legs moving jealous of my husband's sleep as I counted the hours till daybreak. I tried every sleeping pill on the market from natural to over the counter, to pharmaceutical and nothing worked. I had new symptoms as well. I now no longer could hold anything down on my stomach… not even water. It would all come right back up usually with no warning. I began losing weight fast. My mother-in-law stayed with us the first half of December as I was unable to take care of the kids let alone myself and my husband had to work. She recommended I go on walks, which was something my body naturally wanted me to do anyway since it wouldn't let me sit. I lived in a really walkable suburb city of Seattle. If I wasn't walking the streets of the city, it had beautiful little trails through a slight forested area by my house that I could also walk through. Either way I had to cross over a river which is when my suicidal thoughts not induced by medication started to happen. I could just imagine drowning myself in the river to not be a burden to my family. Unbeknownst to me at the time my symptoms were just going to continue to get worse.

My mother-in-law left and my husband was back home. I found my mind reverting back to my childhood and toddler years. Not as in the sense of memories but thought patterns. It was as though at times I would have the brain of a toddler and think that way. I was verging on acting that way as well but retained the adult knowledge to suppress it. It certainly didn't help that I could now no longer talk right and would stutter with every sentence. I also found that periodically my legs would give out from under me making me unable to walk and I was forced to crawl. This further made me feel like I was reverting to a baby and it furthered my suicidal thoughts as well. I remember sitting in our bedroom with one of my husband's machete type knives pointed towards my stomach. My husband walked in and just sat next to me and didn't say or do anything. I sat there for a long while but I couldn't get enough courage to plunge it into my stomach. I eventually sheathed it and put it back in the closet.

My husband had to return to work so he called my sister to come stay with me and the kids. On the way to the Greyhound station to pick her up I pictured jumping out of the car and over the bridge into Lake Washington. Once at the Greyhound station as they were loading my sister's suitcase into the back of the van I saw a commuter train about to pull away from where it was picking up people. I was about to jump out of the van and in front of it when I realized how much it would traumatize my children to see me go out that way so I didn't. It was a long ride back home. The first thing my sister did when she got there was take away my van keys and on outings she would accompany me.

I had little release from my situation. I did find one thing that worked and that was the Benzo. It would relieve my symptoms, but it was short lasting. My body would also grow accustomed to it so I would need higher and higher doses for it to work. My psychiatrist was only allowed to prescribe so high a milligram. I was worried about becoming addicted to it at a level I could no longer achieve so I weaned myself off of it even though it was helping. After five weeks of zero to two hours of sleep a night, my eyes were also incredibly dry. Besides my eyes being constantly open, my tear ducts had quit working. I went to the eye doctor and he prescribed me these really expensive eye drops that even with the best insurance plan we could not afford to buy them. Everywhere we would go if I saw a place where I thought I might be able to end my life I would think about it. Until one day God spoke to my heart and said, "I will heal you so you don't have to think about death anymore."

It was January, my sister had left and I was finally brave enough to go back to the Psychiatrist. I was off the antipsychotic by this point and he prescribed me a new one. Little did I know God's form of healing would come through the hands of a doctor but it did. This new one took away all my negative symptoms I was having and on top of it I was finally able to get a full night's sleep! There were a few drawbacks however. In the first three months I gained 90 pounds and I was also now so tired that after getting the kids to school in the morning I would spend the first half of the day napping. I also was slightly depressed. I was still though relieved because I was back to being myself otherwise. My husband wasn't too happy however because he was picking up chores where I had been slacking due to being tired.

WASHINGTON (PART TWO)

I was on the new antipsychotic for over a year or two and was tired of the weight gain. I ventured to try a new medication. We tried another one which was an immediate nightmare. Probably one of the worst I had tried. Even worse than the "Gray Brain" days of one of my others. I wasn't on it more than a week or two. Then reluctantly, I tried a Seizure medication that works for Bipolar as well. I was hesitant because you have to up the dose very slowly and there is a risk for a life-threatening rash when you go on it. Luckily that didn't happen to me. I found myself pleasantly surprised because my mood was lifted dramatically and I had lots of energy to function. I felt like I could tackle about anything.

We had bought a house at this point and it was summer of 2019. My daughter had me watching a YouTube series with her where the young men explored abandoned places, did pranks, hunted for ghosts, and played with a Ouija Board. She insisted I buy their "Merch", t-shirts and hoodies, and I did for her. One morning in July, the Seattle area experienced an earthquake large enough that it really shook the bed. The thing was in the days that followed the shaking continued. Possible aftershocks I thought. But it continued past the point of aftershocks. I would wake up in the middle of the night and find my bed vibrating. Soon other "events" started taking place in the house. I would hear whispers in my ear at night that I couldn't make out. There would be random thumps on walls and eerie small lights visible in my room. I would wake my husband up it the night but he didn't hear or see anything. I was certain we must have let demons into the house by watching the show with Ouija Boards. I made my daughter quit watching it and had her throw away all her clothes so it wouldn't be an influence to other kids at her school to watch it and have the same thing happen to them. I felt really bad about it because I knew she really wanted them, but she obediently obliged. I started praying the Armor of God over my kids every night with bedtime prayer. I asked them if they had seen anything strange happening around the house. I don't remember what they said, but I do know that one night my daughter called me into her room because her radio was acting strange turning off and on by itself. I sat with her through the night and prayed in tongues which to my surprise in her sleepy state she interpreted. She said, "Mom I think your saying…" and went on to tell me something about a message from God to his little children. She then drifted off to sleep. I asked her about it the next day and she had completely forgotten that she had done that.

About this same time of year, my husband came up to me one day and flat out told me, "I don't love you anymore." and walked away. I just listened and didn't really know what to think but I took it in and continued on with life. I had noticed that Mommy & Daddy time upstairs after the kids were asleep had become less and less. I would stand at the bottom of the stairs and call to him while he was playing video games like I always did but he would never come upstairs with me like he usually did. It was very rare- like once a month. I had a hard time falling asleep without him by my side. He was my pillow and his snoring was like white noise that helped me sleep.

The odd happenings around our house continued happening but my husband was either at work or oblivious to it. I called some friends I knew at the church to come anoint the house with oil and pray over it. One of which even brought her Shofar and blew it in the backyard. I even called the Pastor. He was unable to come over, but did talk to me over the phone. None of it worked.

I was feeling so great at this point with my health that I thought I would apply for a job. I had an interview at a store in the mall but I didn't get the position. It was the beginning of November and mass tragedy struck my extended family that lived in Mexico. I was one of the first to post about it on Facebook requesting prayer. Soon I found my phone ringing off the hook with news reporters wanting the inside scoop. The family in Mexico wanted the US government to intervene to catch the perpetrators so they had asked everyone to reach out to the media, but I had already had the media reaching out to me. I gave the reporters update after update and this went on for days with my husband picking up slack around the house so I could do so. One day I was just arriving home after picking up the kids from school and some take and bake pizza and salad because we had yet to go shopping with all the chaos. It wasn't long before the doorbell rang. It was a social worker from the Department of Children & Family Services. She said there had been allegations made against me and my husband by the school and she needed to interview us and the children. She took the children upstairs one by one to talk to them and I called my husband to come home from work and then began sweeping up cheerios that were strewn across the floor because my kids had been attempting to feed our cats with them. I felt grateful that the rest of the house was clean because I knew she would be inspecting it as well. When she finally came downstairs, she asked me if I had coached the kids on what to say because they had given her perfect answers. I replied to her that I hadn't I was busy sweeping up the cheerios on the floor. She then requested a tour of the house which I gave her. My husband soon came home and she interviewed the two of us together. My mind was reeling at what the accusations could be. She asked us a series of questions and then she got to the one asking if we ever spanked our children. I was always for peaceful parenting but my husband liked to lay down the law and occasionally spank our children. She asked where and he said their butts. To my relief she said this was fine as long as it was the only part of their bodies he hit and it was only done with an open hand. Once her questions ended, she revealed that the allegations were that the school couldn't get my kids to behave in class which she said was on them and not us and that we must be starving our children because they could never get them to touch their food in school. She asked to see the inside of the fridge- the one thing I had forgotten to show her. I explained to her that I had our kids eating fruits and vegetables and it was working until one day my husband introduced them to Ramen Noodles and that was for the most part all they would eat from that day forward. I showed her that our pantry and freezer were full of foods and the reason why was that they were foods the kids didn't like so they wouldn't touch them. I showed her that the refrigerator was empty except for the pizzas and salads I had just bought because we were due for a shopping trip for the foods my kids did like to eat. That ended her visit and with that she said goodbye and left telling us it would be a while for her to finish her investigational findings. We took our kids to the doctor afterwards so we could have the doctor send the social worker a report on the health of our children. The Pediatrician said we had no worries that our children looked perfectly healthy and well cared for and she would forward her findings to the social worker. I still worried though because the case had yet to be closed.

One day I came across an article about emotional abuse online. It stated that people don't intentionally get into an emotionally abusive relationship. That it is like a faucet that drips and drips and drips until one day the sink overflows. It had a list of traits of an emotionally abusive relationship and there were just too many checks I could check off on the list that matched my relationship for my comfort with the main one being treated like a wallflower. I was constantly being treated like I was not there when I was in a room with my husband. I would have to call his name multiple times to even have him answer a question for me. When he came home, I confronted him with the list. I told him that only God could help him change. I didn't know it at the time but the stress from Child Protective Services visit was causing me to go manic. When he only became angry at my request and didn't improve after the next week's timeframe but got worse, I asked him for a divorce… and my daughter was in the same room when I did. I was manic and thought I was capable of doing anything without him. He didn't love me anyway- he had told me so. It was November 19th and I hadn't even given him enough time to change, even though he would later end up improving.

The devil was in the works. I wasn't actively seeking to date anybody or even thinking about it but a man from Africa messaged me on Facebook. His name was Kingsley. He told me he had had a dream about me and he told me it. Everything he told me confirmed that he had been shown things about my life he shouldn't know. He even knew about my situation with my husband and said that God had sent him to me to take care of me now and be my new husband. I just accepted it even though he wasn't a very attractive man because I figured it was God bringing him to me. He was an architect and made beautiful houses in Nigeria. I continued conversing with him over the next few weeks. We made plans together to marry and he mailed me a Bible, white handkerchiefs, and an engagement ring with the last of his money. I was becoming ever increasingly more delusional. I was getting my nails done at the nail salon one day and fell asleep three times while the technician was doing my nails. She kept asking me if I was ok. I assured her I was. When I was done there, I found myself falling asleep at a stop light. I was sure I was under attack by a demon that could control sleep. In my psychosis, I drove and drove and drove trying to outdrive this sleep demon and with a new found African dialect of tongues I was casting it out as I went paying no attention to my speed or the battery level of the GPS on my phone. Luckily, I was on a little used highway as this was occurring. As I entered the city, I was declaring that God had given me dominion over this part of the city and that and that the demon had no right to be there. My phone eventually died and I lost my GPS having no charger with me. I drove until I had to get fuel. I stopped at a gas station and saw a homeless man. I could sense Jesus sitting in the passenger seat and I knew what I had to do. I went in and bought the man some food and brought it out to him. Then I went back inside to ask for directions to one of the local beaches. When I went back outside the homeless man was gone and I "knew" it was Jesus and he had disappeared. I fueled up and drove to the beach following the directions the gas station attendant had given me. On my way I passed a bench that overlooked the water so I pulled off to the side of the road and got out of the van. I sat on the bench and noticed a still sealed bottle of water. It was like God had left it there just for me. So, I enjoyed the views as I sipped the water. When I was through, I continued onto the marina and beach. As I looked at all the boats docked in the marina I began to cry. I just had this overwhelming knowing that my husband was going to commit suicide. I could envision him hanging himself from our light fixture which was attached to our seventeen-foot ceilings. I cried and cried as I mourned a loss that was yet to come. When the tears stopped flowing, I made my way back to the van. I headed home and somehow miraculously made it with not a clue as to where I was directionally. My husband was at home waiting and I told him that I was worried about him committing suicide and what I had envisioned. He just listened. Later I talked to Kingsley online and told him about the geographical territories God was giving me and I didn't really believe it but I asked him if he thought I could be the Queen of the South spoken of in the Bible. He said that he indeed thought I was. That made me think I was too. The Lamictal had a side effect that made my body incredibly itchy especially my arms and my scalp, but I had been doing so well on it I stayed on it. I had sores on my arms from scratching so much and one day it seemed they had suddenly cleared up. I thought that God was finally healing me from all of my diseases and I even proclaimed the miracle online. I was so certain of it I quit taking all of my medications. It only took about a week for all my symptoms to start up and I immediately went back on my meds, realized I hadn't been healed, and had the greater than that knowledge that this whole thing was demons in the works! Kingsley- all of it! I called off his proposal, mailed him back the ring, Bible, and handkerchiefs with an additional $500.00 for his trouble. He was weeping. He would later inform me that the Nigerian customs had taken the ring and money and left him with a torn-up Bible. There was nothing I could do about it and I wanted him out of my life, so I blocked him.

I spent my free time shopping for furniture for my future apartment both online and in person. In a few weeks' time, I had purchased $15,000 worth on credit card which I stored in the garage. My husband thought my spending was out of control and as soon as I would bring things in or they would arrive by mail he would sort through them with me and would return what he thought was unnecessary. It was mid-December and as I was online one day my Facebook page suddenly went viral. I had an appointment that was going to last all day that day to get my haired dyed in peacock colors at the hair salon. As I sat there in the hair dresser's chair the notifications on my phone were going off like wild. The hair dresser across the way got sick of hearing it and asked me if I could put my phone on silent. I apologized and told her my page had suddenly gone viral. When I got home, I posted my new hairstyle on Facebook and accepted friend request after friend request. Soon my page was full with the maximum 5,000 friends I could have and I had a couple hundred followers. Most of the people were from around the world but especially from Africa. A lot of them were Christian and I reposted post after inspirational post I could find. My cousin who was a nurse and had worked Psych saw my activity online and notified my sister that my posting was overly manic when in fact I had just gone viral. My sister than notified my husband that I was manic. I was mad at my cousin and blocked her. After I blocked her, I got a phone call from her brother swearing at me that I was out of my mind and about to lose my family. I blocked him as well. Neither of them knew what I was going through in my marriage. It didn't take long before my family and original friends on Facebook were receiving friend requests from my new global friends online. They found it annoying and asked if I could make it stop. One by one I blocked each of my global friends. However, this was not before I had come across this rapper's page that intrigued me. I am a huge fan of rap music. I got to talking to him and I really liked his stuff even though it was in a language I couldn't understand. The more we talked the more we hit it off until we were talking to each other night and day on video call. His name was Samba.

The paranormal continued in my house and just like the Sleep Demon, it was now following me out of the house as well. I was at the grocery store once and all but three of the freezer doors in the freezer aisle opened on their own and shut again. That really freaked me out. I looked around and there was only one other person in the aisle and she didn't see it happen. At night I would wonder who I was supposed to be with next and a circle of three to four men rotated though my head. I just didn't know which one. One of them however was God. I knew He didn't have a wife and I lay there feeling very sorry for Him. Perhaps I was to be God's wife. I pictured the whiteness of God's light and then my darkness and thought that just maybe the two could co-exist. Black & White- Yin & Yang.

One day as things progressed with Samba, I decided I was going to sell my wedding ring. I took it to the jewelry store and I misheard them. I thought they said they could give me $600 but they actually had said $60. I knew we had bought it for $4,000 but I had reluctantly agreed. I gave them the ring and they gave me a check. It took about a week for my husband to find out what I had done and we agreed together that I had gotten a bad deal so we returned to the jewelry store saying we wanted to reconcile our marriage and could they get it back for us. It was on its way to a Denver processing center to be broken down into reclaimed metal. They were able to call them though and have it mailed back and I returned to them the check they had written. After this my husband and I actually started talking about reconciling. My mania ruined it though, because one night I was downstairs talking to Samba on the phone and my mania went wild I couldn't shut up. Words kept flowing out of my mouth at rapid speed. I asked Samba if he thought I was going manic to which he replied he thought I was fine. My husband came downstairs however and heard the conversation with Samba and gave me this heartbroken look. My manic conversation continued into the night as well as the next morning. My husband came downstairs and told me that was it he was taking me to the E.R. It was January. He took me to a different hospital than the one I had been at before so they were unfamiliar with my record. The hospital itself didn't have a Psych Ward so they were going to transfer me to a behavioral clinic. While we were waiting, he told me to forget about Samba. When I was in a room by myself, I defiantly wrote down

Samba's contact information on a paper and put it in my purse so I wouldn't forget. When the ambulance arrived to take me to the clinic, they asked me if there was any particular song I wanted them to play on the ride and I requested Samba's rap music. I must have blacked out because I don't recall arriving to the behavioral unit. I remember standing outside my room there's door turning in slow circles with hazy thoughts going through my head as I wasn't really with it or observing the things around me but my brain alone. I would later be told that I stood there in one spot for 24 hours straight until they forced me into bed. I then spent the next day Catatonic in bed as well. Thoughts about the origins of the Universe looping through my head from front to back and over and over again. I stared only at the shapes on the ceiling grate with my only movements being my left thumb circling around the tip of my ring finger over and over again as if to say I should be married with a ring on that finger. Doctors and nurses would come by my bedside but I would barely if at all notice as I was in a haze. I only could feel the pinprick of a nurse giving me a shot.

The next day I came to and there was a doctor in another room who wanted to talk to me. I could barely talk, but I knew it was important to give him a list of all the medications I had had aversions to so I wouldn't have to repeat any past side effects. He told me how I was barely with it yesterday and it was good to see me finally up. One of the nurses told me that it was state law that all people in the clinic be given a shot if they refused to or were unable to take their medication. I don't know what the shot was but I figured it was to subdue them. I found out this clinic was not only for Psych patients but drug rehab as well.

I don't have too many remarkable memories with this clinic. For the most part the days just dragged on and on. It was the worst of the clinics aesthetically I had been to. None of the bathrooms in the rooms had doors just a curtain so the hallways often smelled unpleasant. I remember one day everybody was headed to the gym for some recreation time and I got up to go and they said, "Except for you. You can't leave." I still to this day don't know why except for maybe I was a fall hazard with my mobility issues. There was a patient in the clinic who looked just like

Adam Sandler and I told him so. I thought he was cool to hang out with but he was often with a different group of friends. I really only had one friend in this clinic and it was a girl whose boyfriend had just died and so she checked herself in due to sadness and grief. She was an exotic dancer and I loved to dance so we got along great. I would talk to her about meeting up to dance or take lessons together after we got out so we exchanged phone numbers. Unfortunately, I ended up losing her number when I got out before I had the chance to call her. The Psychiatrist in this clinic ended up choosing a First-Generation psych drug combined with a mood stabilizer to treat me. I assumed this was because I was having so much bad luck with the Second-Generation medications. I was in this behavioral unit for two weeks and then my husband picked me up.

After getting out of the clinic and returning home, I noticed that all my issues with demons was gone. It turns out I had just been hallucinating them for the past seven months while living an almost fully functional lifestyle. I still had a long way to go on my recovery this time and unfortunately Samba was one of the first people I contacted when I got home because I knew he had no idea where I was the last two weeks. One thing that was resolved was the social worker contacted us letting us know she had dropped the allegations against us and her investigation had found us to be fit parents. I did find myself not as happy and lively as I had been when I was on the Seizure med and the depression would get to me over the next few months.

My conversations continued on night and day with Samba by video phone. I eventually booked plane tickets to go see him in The Gambia and started packing. My vacation plans however were interrupted by the Covid lockdown when they shut down all flights. My husband started working from home and my conversations continued with Samba.

I believe it was an unfortunate day in April, my husband and I were fighting- not physically, but verbally. In the heat of the moment, I rashly decided to sign the divorce papers we had ready. My head was still not healed completely from my mental breakdown at this point either. It would take me about nine months after that January behavioral clinic stay to feel fully myself. I would find myself often going back and forth between wanting to pick my husband and wanting to pick Samba. I was feeling loved by Samba and I wasn't by my husband. I think I was just looking and waiting for him to love me and give me attention like Samba did. This undecided mental dance would continue the rest of the summer.

In June I finally saw a sleep doctor that had been booked for half a year. I was diagnosed with Severe Sleep Apnea. This would explain me falling asleep all the time at random places during the day. Not a sleep demon! I should have taken home a CPAP machine to help my breathing while I sleep, but I was afraid of it being unsexy so I didn't. This would be another thing I would come to regret down the line. I still don't have one to this day I am writing this and wish I did. I would also see my personal psychiatrist this same June. He didn't agree that the seizure med was causing me to hallucinate. He said I had been doing well the seven months I was hallucinating demons, but I also hadn't told him about it because I thought it was a spiritual problem and not a mental one. The med helped with my depression however so we agreed I should add it to my other medications at half the dose I had been taking. This also helped with the itching it gave me. Only my head seemed itchy from time to time instead of my whole body. In June my body was still recovering from my breakdown and had noticeable movement issues especially walking.

In July I insisted my husband and I take marriage counseling. Instead of the family counselor we had used once before that I liked, we had to go with one his insurance covered. I did not like this lady. She was very partial and would side with my husband a lot. I felt like she was more for divorce than reconciling our marriage. My husband would often say, "I have one foot in this marriage and one foot out." Instead of me finally deciding between Samba or my husband, my husband made the final decision without me. He decided he wanted out of the marriage. He's the one that pulled the plug. We didn't even finish counseling. I felt cheated out of making a decision. Inwardly I wanted to stay married. In the months that followed I would beg him to take me back and he would refuse saying I already signed the divorce papers.

There were no in person court hearings for the divorce because of the lockdown. My husband had and attorney and I did not. Come October 2020 our divorce was finalized. My now ex-husband brought home a cake with the words divorced written across the top of it to break the news to me. I couldn't blame him, he took a play out of my own book, I had once bought a similar cake for an employee the company I worked for told me I needed to fire. I wanted to break it to him gently. About this same time of year, I broke up with Samba. It turned out he was good boyfriend material, but not good husband material. Now I had neither my husband or Samba.

I continued to live in our family home until January when I got my own apartment. I couldn't afford the mortgage payment on the house so my ex got the house in the divorce which means he also got the kids except for every other weekend, summers, & winter break. I rationalized that it would be hard for everybody if I made them live in a one-bedroom apartment with me. I also didn't want to take the kids away from the friends they had made at school.

It wouldn't be long until I installed a free online dating app on my phone. I found someone I thought lived in Seattle, but I was so wrong. Unbeknownst to me I had started an online relationship with an African scammer. Within three to four months all the money I had won in my divorce settlement was gone. He had told me he needed it to pay taxes on a much larger amount of money his new job was giving him before they would release the funds to him. Then once he had the money, he would travel to America and we would get married. It was all a relationship scam. I reported him to the FBI but never got any of my money back.

At this point I continued to live off of credit cards and alimony checks until I started working in May. I hadn't had a job in twelve years since I had been a stay-at-home mom. I figured childcare would be the most logical job for me to get into without recent job experience. I was supposed to be the assistant teacher at a daycare, but with a shortage of childcare workers they made me the main teacher of the two- and three-year-old class and it was a full class load. The toddlers were constantly climbing up on the toddler size furniture and biting and hitting each other. I was afraid one of them was going to get injured on my watch. My sleep apnea also wanted to kick in during nap time when the lights were off in the classroom. I knew I needed to find a different job.

About two to three months into the daycare job, I was hired by a lawncare company. Initially I was to inspect peoples' properties for insect damage, but I felt uncomfortable with that so they put me on phones. I did really good the first summer selling pest control. Sleep Apnea was still an issue though as I would nod off occasionally on the computer.

My kids would come to visit me every other weekend because I was working. They were unhappy with the small quarters & lack of internet connection and would often complain about it. I would try to get them to get out of the apartment and do other fun things with me but they just didn't want to. My daughter would soon refuse to visit me anymore and this has continued to be the case to this day. She has a hatred of me since the divorce. Not only did I lose my husband with the divorce but I lost my daughter as well. My son (now Trans), although he didn't hate me, he hated that I didn't have internet and also refused to see me but stayed in contact over Discord. My twins continued to be happy to see me and would visit me every other weekend.

I had now started dating in person as well as online and went through several relationships. A few of them wanted to marry me and I just wasn't interested. The ones I wanted to marry weren't interested in me. I continued to beg my ex-husband to take me back to no avail. At the end of the year, he started dating again and at the beginning of 2022 he found a girlfriend. I was heartbroken all over again.

Come summer, although my mental health was fine, I was still having issues with my Sleep Apnea. My boss gave me an ultimatum that I needed to get it taken care of or he would have to fire me. I talked to my biological mom and she told me she would help me cover the cost of a CPAP machine. I told my boss this and he was satisfied. However, I ended up having car trouble and had to use the CPAP money for car repairs. In the end, my pest control sales that I excelled at the first year tanked and they fired me. I really wasn't doing anything different but I think it was due to a downed economy.

My apartment lease was now up for renewal and I had no job, only alimony, and no credit cards because they had been maxed out. I was actually in the process of filing bankruptcy because of my debt. I didn't know where I was going to go because rent is extremely high in Seattle and I didn't make much in alimony. My biological mom wanted to take me in but her elderly husband was afraid he would catch Covid if anyone lived with them. It was looking like I would be living out of my car. Thankfully that didn't happen and my biological dad had a really old trailer in Texas that he said I could live in. So, I drove to Texas.

While I lived in Texas, I started going to Abundant church and rededicated my life to God. I had backslidden and been blaming God for my divorce. I knew he had brought me and my husband together and I knew it was supposed to be for forever, so I just didn't understand how it could end especially with all my praying for reconciliation. In Christianity marriage is a symbol of Christ and His Church. Christ doesn't leave His Church; He loves His Church. A man is supposed to love his wife like Christ loves the Church and mine didn't do that. I couldn't reconcile this in my head as to why it ended.

I would make a few friends while I was in Texas and more importantly, I got to see my biological dad and three of my half siblings as well as nieces and nephews! I definitely enjoyed a warmer winter than I'm used to. I would end up living there for a total of nine months. I kept in touch with my Trans child (I would say daughter but since she has an older sister it's just easier to distinguish them in this book by saying Trans child) on Discord and my Twins on video call. As much as I tried to contact my daughter she would never reply.

In March of 2023, my biological mom's husband died and she asked me to come live with her. I had to wrap up doctor's appointments and get some more prescriptions before I could leave for Utah to live with her. It was the end of May when I finally arrived.

Two weeks later in June, I found out that my ex-husband was getting married to his girlfriend. I was again crushed. What's more I felt like she was stealing all my hard work in addition to my husband. My ex-husband was a carpenter when I met him. I suggested he go to an IT job fair. He did and landed an IT job. I was with him supporting him the whole time he worked up in his career. We went from barely making it to finally had made it just a few years before the divorce. With four kids on top of it! We had been married fifteen years! I felt like she was swooping in and profiting from the years of all my labor and undeservingly. What's even worse is some of my kids started calling her "mom" after this! I'm the one that nearly died due to delivery complications- this is supposed to be my title and my title alone! How dare she disrupt my world.

In July I did get the privilege of all four kids visiting me and my biological mom for two weeks. The only reason my daughter came was because my ex and his new wife (how I hate calling her that) were selling the house and had open houses. Yeah, that one- the one I let him keep so the kids could keep their friends. So much for that happening! Except for my daughter the other three kids enjoyed their time here. I felt sad as I had to fly them back to Seattle. I was quite depressed for months after they left just because I missed my kids and my life felt empty again.

The next seven months and counting would be spent with my biological mom. My Sleep Apnea continues and I find myself napping throughout the day. My mental health is good. It took me trying seven different medications before I found the combination that works for me. It's been four years since I've been in a Psych Ward. I am hopeful that my mental stability will continue. It is currently the month of February 2024. I get my very last alimony check this month. I hope to eventually get my sleep apnea sorted out and return to work. I also hope that I will find the love of my life that loves me like Christ loves His Church. I pray that I will get a place of my own where my kids can live with me. And I pray that one day my daughter will forgive me and reconcile with me.

PARTING WORDS

I hope those who have read this book find hope. My hope is found in Christ and He can be found by just believing in Him. He came to forgive us of our sins, bring us health, and give us life more abundantly. I suggest reading your Bible, watching inspiring sermons on YouTube, going to church, finding a close friend group in church, and being baptized by water as well as the Holy Spirit. Jesus will become not only your savior but your friend.

Although I had a lot of side effects with medication, I also found them necessary in my mental health journey. Also note that not everyone is going to have the same side effects I did on the medications I was on because everybody is different. Don't be ashamed to find help from a doctor too. I pray that whoever reads this will be well.

God Bless,

Jade Nicoletti

About the Author

Jade Nicoletti is an author and mother to four beautiful children (including identical twins) ages seventeen, sixteen, twelve, and twelve. She currently resides in Utah. She was born into a Fundamentalist Mormon family background and found Jesus Christ and realized Mormonism was a cult at age nineteen. She enjoys reading, writing, listening to music, coffee shops, cafés, warm sunny beaches with palm trees, and watching sermons on YouTube.

Dear Reader,

I'm writing this book to make the subject of mental health less taboo. I figured if I come out with my personal experience of being hospitalized in the Psychiatric Ward not only once, but four times, people in a similar dilemma will be able to relate and hopefully find camaraderie, if not comfort. It is important that this subject becomes destigmatized so that those suffering from it can be treated like any other patient suffering from any other disease. It is sad to see what people diagnosed with a mental illness have to go through, other than the illness itself, because of misconceptions. I hope people reading this book will get a real dose of what it is like.

Sincerely,

Jade Nicoletti

www.ingramcontent.com/pod-product-compliance
Lightning Source LLC
Chambersburg PA
CBHW061247250726
48653CB00002B/553